Retro Tech Riches: Thrifting and Selling Vintage Electronics

By Silas Meadowlark

Index

- Introduction to Retro Tech Thrifting
  - The Allure of Vintage Electronics
  - Understanding the Retro Tech Market
  - Preparing for Your Thrifting Journey

- Essential Tools and Equipment
  - Necessary Gadgets and Accessories
  - Safely Handling Vintage Electronics
  - Cleaning and Restoring Techniques

- Identifying Valuable Vintage Electronics
  - Recognizing Classic Brands and Models
  - Assessing Condition and Functionality
  - Researching Pricing and Demand

- Thrifting Strategies for Retro Tech
  - Scouring Thrift Stores and Garage Sales
  - Online Hunting for Hidden Gems
  - Networking with Collectors and Enthusiasts

- Storing and Preserving Your Finds
  - Proper Packaging and Transportation
  - Climate-Controlled Storage Solutions
  - Maintaining the Integrity of Your Collection

- Researching and Pricing Your Inventory
  - Utilizing Online Resources and Price Guides
  - Evaluating Rarity and Collectibility
  - Determining the Right Selling Price

- Selling on Online Marketplaces
  - Setting Up Selling Accounts and Profiles
  - Crafting Effective Listings and Descriptions

- Managing Shipping and Customer Service
- Selling at Retro Tech Fairs and Conventions
  - Navigating Vendor Applications and Fees
  - Presenting and Displaying Your Items
  - Engaging with Buyers and Collectors
- Building Your Retro Tech Brand
  - Developing a Unique Selling Proposition
  - Leveraging Social Media and Online Presence
  - Fostering a Loyal Customer Base
- Scaling Your Retro Tech Business
  - Expanding Your Inventory and Sourcing
  - Automating and Streamlining Processes
  - Diversifying Your Product Offerings
- Navigating Legal and Tax Considerations
  - Understanding Seller Regulations and Licenses
  - Properly Reporting Income and Expenses
  - Protecting Yourself from Liability
- Outsourcing and Partnerships
  - Leveraging Dropshipping and Fulfillment Services
  - Collaborating with Repair Specialists
  - Forging Mutually Beneficial Relationships
- Maintaining a Sustainable Retro Tech Business
  - Adapting to Market Trends and Changes
  - Preventing Burnout and Stress Management
  - Reinvesting and Diversifying Your Income Streams
- Giving Back to the Retro Tech Community
  - Sharing Knowledge and Expertise
  - Organizing Workshops and Meetups
  - Supporting Preservation and Restoration Efforts
- Conclusion and Future Outlook
  - Embracing the Passion for Retro Tech

- Exploring Emerging Opportunities
- Continuing Your Entrepreneurial Journey

Introduction to Retro Tech Thrifting

The Allure of Vintage Electronics

In a world consumed by sleek, minimalist design and disposable gadgets, there's a growing subset of tech enthusiasts who find themselves drawn to the alluring world of vintage electronics. These analog relics, with their tactile controls, warm displays, and undeniable charm, have captured the hearts and minds of a new generation of collectors and entrepreneurs. Whether it's the nostalgic pull of a beloved childhood toy or the thrill of unearthing a rare, coveted find, the lure of retro tech is a siren's call that's impossible to ignore.

Picture this: you're rummaging through a dusty thrift store, your fingers tracing the familiar curves of a vintage radio, its dial illuminated by a soft amber glow. The weight of the device in your hands, the satisfying click of the tuning knob - it's a sensory experience that transcends the purely functional. These vintage marvels aren't just tools; they're time capsules, windows into a bygone era when technology was as much a work of art as it was a practical solution.

But the allure of retro tech extends beyond mere aesthetics. There's an innate sense of satisfaction in reviving these forgotten relics, in breathinglife back into them and witnessing them come alive once more. It's a challenge, a puzzle to be solved, and the joy of the hunt is only eclipsed by the pride of restoring a piece of history to its former glory.

Understanding the Retro Tech Market

As the demand for vintage electronics continues to grow, so too does the intricacy of the retro tech market. This is a terrain defined by a unique blend of nostalgia, scarcity, and the ever evolving preferences of a diverse collector base. From the die hard enthusiasts seeking out rare, pristine specimens to the casual hobbyists looking to add a touch of vintage charm to their modern lives, the retro tech market is a dynamic and ever changing environment.

Understanding the nuances of this market is important for anyone looking to start on a successful thrifting and reselling journey. Factors such as brand recognition, model rarity, condition, and historical significance all play a role in determining the value of a vintage electronic item. It's a delicate balance of art and science, where knowledge and research can mean the difference between a lucrative find and a disappointing dead end.

But the rewards for those who navigate this market with skill and savvy are substantial. The thrill of discovering a hidden gem, the satisfaction of restoring it to its former glory, and the financial rewards that come with selling to a passionate collector base – these are the hallmarks of a thriving retro tech business. And as the market continues to evolve, the opportunities for those willing to dive in and embrace the challenge only grow more tantalizing.

Preparing for Your Thrifting Journey

Starting on a successful retro tech thrifting adventure requires more than just a keen eye and a love for vintage gadgets. It's a journey that demands preparation, research, and a willingness to step outside your comfort zone. The first step is to immerse yourself in the world of retro tech, familiarizing yourself with the classic brands, models, and design trends that have defined the industry over the decades.

Scour online forums, collector communities, and price guides to gain a deeper understanding of the market's ebbs and flows. Learn to spot the telltale signs of a valuable find, from the distinctive styling of a Braun radio to the unmistakable heft of a vintage Walkman. Equip yourself with the knowledge to navigate thrift stores, garage sales, and online marketplaces like a seasoned pro, separating the hidden gems from the items best left behind.

But preparation extends beyond mere research – it's also about cultivating the right mindset. Retro tech thrifting is not for the faint of heart; it requires a combination of patience, persistence, and a willingness to embrace the unexpected. Be prepared to sift through countless unremarkable items, to negotiate with eager sellers, and to occasionally come up empty handed. The true thrill lies in the hunt, in the challenge of unearthing those coveted treasures that will captivate collectors and enthusiasts alike.

Essential Tools and Equipment

Necessary Gadgets and Accessories

Initiating on your retro tech thrifting journey requires more than just a keen eye and a passion for vintage electronics. To truly succeed in this endeavor, you'll need to arm yourself with the right tools and equipment. Think of it as assembling your very own superheroine utility belt, except instead of batarangs and grappling hooks, you'll be packing multimeters, soldering irons, and a whole lot of elbow grease.

First and foremost, a reliable multimeter is an absolute must have. This nifty little device will become your trusty sidekick, allowing you to diagnose the health and functionality of any vintage electronics you come across. Don't be intimidated by the seemingly complex array of knobs and buttons – with a little practice, you'll be wielding that multimeter like a true pro, ready to uncover the secrets hidden within those dusty old components.

Next on the list, a good soldering iron is an indispensable tool for any retro tech enthusiast. Whether you're repairing a vintage radio or breathinglife back into a classic Walkman, your soldering skills will be put to the test. Invest in a quality soldering iron that can handle the delicate work required for these detailed devices. And don't forget the solder itself – the right alloy can make all the difference in achieving a clean, reliable connection.

Speaking of cleaning, a comprehensive toolkit for restoring vintage electronics is essential. This includes a set of precision screwdrivers, tweezers, and a can of compressed air to dislodge those pesky dust bunnies that have made themselves at home inside your treasured finds. Don't forget the all important demagnetizer, which will help you rid those CRT displays of any unwanted magnetic interference.

Finally, consider investing in a few storage solutions to keep your burgeoning collection of retro tech gems in pristine condition. Antistatic bags, bubble wrap, and sturdy containers will ensure that your prized possessions remain safe and sound during transport and storage. After all, you wouldn't want to risk those vintage components falling victim to the dreaded static shock or a wayward shipping mishap.

Safely Handling Vintage Electronics

Handling vintage electronics requires a delicate touch and a keen awareness of potential hazards. These relics from a bygone era were not built to the same safety standards as modern devices, so it's essential to approach them with the utmost care and caution.

First and foremost, always unplug any vintage electronics before attempting to work on them. You'd be surprised how much residual charge can linger in those old capacitors, and a wayward finger could spell disaster for both you and your prized possession. When in doubt, discharge those pesky caps using a proper resistor based discharging tool to ensure your safety.

Speaking of safety, don't forget the importance of personal protective equipment (PPE) when delving into the world of retro tech. A sturdy pair of gloves can help shield your hands from sharp edges and unexpected shocks, while a pair of safety glasses will guard your eyes from any flying debris or errant solder splatter.

And let's not forget about the potential for toxic materials lurking within those vintage devices. Many older electronics contained substances like lead, mercury, and even asbestos, which can pose serious health risks if mishandled. Always exercise caution when disassembling or repairing any questionable vintage items, and consider seeking professional assistance if you're not confident in your ability to handle the situation safely.

Remember, safety should always be your top priority when working with retro tech. By taking the necessary precautions and investing in the right protective gear, you'll be able to explore the world of vintage electronics with peace of mind, ensuring that your passion for the past doesn't come at the cost of your well being.

Cleaning and Restoring Techniques

Bringing a vintage electronic device back to its former glory is a labor of love, and the key to success lies in your cleaning and restoration techniques. These old school marvels have weathered the test of time, and with a little TLC, you can help them shine once again.

First and foremost, always start with a thorough exterior cleaning. Use a mild, non abrasive cleaner and a soft cloth to gently wipe away any accumulated dust, grime, and tarnish. Be especially mindful of delicate surfaces, like the complicated dials and buttons that add so much character to these vintage gems.

Next, it's time to tackle the interior. Carefully disassemble the device, taking note of each screw, clip, and connector to ensure a smooth reassembly. Use a can of compressed air to dislodge any stubborn dust and debris, being careful not to disturb any sensitive components. For tougher buildup, a soft bristled brush can work wonders, but always exercise caution to avoid any accidental damage.

When it comes to restoring the inner workings, your soldering skills will come into play. Inspect each circuit board, capacitor, and connection, and be prepared to replace any faulty or deteriorating parts. Don't be afraid to dive deep into the guts of these vintage marvels – with a little patience and a steady hand, you can breathe new life into even the most neglected devices.

Once the cleaning and repairs are complete, it's time to focus on preserving your newly revived treasure. Consider applying a protective coating or sealant to the exterior to guard against future wear and tear. And don't forget about proper storage – those climate controlled conditions you set up earlier will be vital in maintaining the integrity of your retro tech collection for years to come.

Restoring vintage electronics is a true labor of love, but the satisfaction of bringing these technological relics back to life is unparalleled. With the right tools, a keen eye for detail, and a healthy dose of elbow grease, you'll be well on your way to transforming your thrifted finds into retro tech treasures that will dazzle and delight collectors and enthusiasts alike.

Identifying Valuable Vintage Electronics

Recognizing Classic Brands and Models

Ah, the thrill of the hunt! When it comes to vintage electronics, recognizing the classic brands and models is key to uncovering the hidden treasures that could bring you riches beyond your wildest dreams. It's like being a treasure hunter, sifting through the sands of time to uncover long lost relics that could be worth a fortune. But fear not, my fellow retro tech enthusiasts, for we shall guide you through the labyrinth of vintage electronics and help you become a veritable Sherlock Holmes of the thrifting world.

First and foremost, familiarize yourself with the hallmark brands that have stood the test of time. Names like Sony, Panasonic, Atari, and Commodore are the holy grail of vintage electronics, commanding the attention of collectors and enthusiasts alike. But don't sleep on the lesser known gems – sometimes, the most valuable finds are hiding in plain sight, like a pristine Zenith radio or a mint condition Magnavox Odyssey console.

And let's not forget the iconic models that have become the stuff of legend. The Walkman, the Polaroid camera, the Nintendo Entertainment System – these are the relics that evoke a sense of nostalgia and command a premium price on the secondary market. Keep your eyes peeled for these legendary devices, and be ready to pounce when you spot them in the wild.

Assessing Condition and Functionality

Now, let's talk about the nitty gritty of evaluating your vintage electronics finds. Condition is everything, my friends, and you need to be a detecting eye to separate the gems from the junk. Start by giving the item a thorough inspection, checking for any signs of damage, wear, or neglect. A pristine, untouched device will fetch a far higher price than one that's been through the ringer.

But condition is only half the battle – you also need to ensure the item is fully functional. That vintage Walkman might look like it just rolled off the assembly line, but if the cassette mechanism is on the fritz, it's not going to be worth much to a collector. Bring along a small toolkit and be prepared to test the item's various features and functions. Don't be afraid to get your hands dirty and dive into the inner workings – you never know what hidden treasures you might uncover.

Remember, the key to assessing condition and functionality is to approach each item with a critical eye, but also with a touch of reverence. These are not just items to be bought and sold – they are time capsules, windows into a bygone era that we're privileged to experience. Treat them with the care and respect they deserve, and you'll be well on your way to uncovering the true value of your vintage finds.

Researching Pricing and Demand

Ah, the sweet smell of success – the moment when you uncover a vintage gem and realize it could be worth a small fortune. But before you start dreaming of the riches that await, it's time to do your homework and really understand the market.

First and foremost, dive into the world of online price guides and collector forums. These are the is a rich source of information that will help you navigate the ever changing scene of vintage electronics pricing. From eBay sold listings to specialized collector databases, these resources will give you a solid understanding of what your find is truly worth.

But it's not just about the price tag – you also need to consider the demand. Is this a sought after item that collectors are clamoring for, or is it a more niche product with a smaller audience? Research the collector community, find out what's hot and what's not, and position your offering accordingly.

And don't forget the power of networking! Reach out to fellow retro tech enthusiasts, join online communities, and tap into the collective knowledge of those who have been in the game for years. You never know when a chance encounter might uncover a hidden gem or lead you to a lucrative partnership.

Remember, pricing and demand are the keys to making accessible the true value of your vintage finds. With a little elbow grease and a lot of savvy research, you'll be well on your way to maximizing your profits and cementing your reputation as a retro tech mogul. So get out there, dig deep, and let the hunt begin!

Thrifting Strategies for Retro Tech

Scouring Thrift Stores and Garage Sales

Ahh, the thrill of the hunt! Thrifting for retro tech is like starting on a treasure seeking adventure, where the potential payoff is a vintage gem that could make you a small fortune. But let me tell you, it's not for the faint of heart. You've got to be willing to dig through piles of dusty electronics, dodge the occasional wayward shopping cart, and navigate the treacherous maze of knick knacks and tchotchkes. But trust me, when you stumble upon that pristine Commodore 64 or a mint condition Walkman, the rush is unbeatable.

Now, don't be fooled by the seemingly innocuous nature of these thrift store and garage sale haunts. These are battlegrounds where the true retro tech warriors clash, engaging in a high stakes game of find the-hidden gem. You've got to have your wits about you, a keen eye for detail, and a willingness to get your hands dirty (literally and figuratively). Scan every nook and cranny, examine every tangled cord and tarnished metal surface. Who knows, that unassuming VCR could be the key to uncovering your retro tech riches.

And let's not forget the art of negotiation. These thrift store denizens are no pushovers – they know the value of their wares, and they'll drive a hard bargain. But that's where your powers of persuasion come into play. Charm them with your infectious enthusiasm, dazzle them with your extensive knowledge of vintage electronics, and don't be afraid to haggle like a seasoned pro. Remember, the true victory lies in walking away with that coveted piece of tech at a price that'll make your accountant do a double take.

Online Hunting for Hidden Gems

Now, I know what you're thinking – "Isn't the thrill of thrifting all about the hunt, the physical interaction with dusty boxes and musty basements?" Well, my friend, you're not wrong. But in this digital age, the online realm has become a veritable rich source for the retro tech enthusiast. Think of it as a global garage sale, where the rare and the obscure lurk just out of sight, waiting to be discovered by the savvy and the persistent.

Start by scouring the depths of online marketplaces like eBay, Craigslist, and Facebook Marketplace. These digital hunting grounds are teeming with hidden gems, from vintage game consoles to one of-a kind audio equipment. But don't just stop there – dive into the niche forums and collector communities, where the real insiders share their secrets and tip each other off to the latest finds. It's like having a personal network of retro tech spies, all working to uncover the most elusive and valuable pieces.

Of course, online hunting comes with its own set of challenges. Navigating the sea of listings, distinguishing between the gems and the duds, and ensuring the authenticity of your finds – it's a delicate balancing act. But fear not, my fellow retro tech enthusiasts, for with a little practice and a lot of research, you'll be snagging those rare and coveted items with the skill of a seasoned cyber scavenger.

Networking with Collectors and Enthusiasts

In the world of retro tech, it's not just about what you know – it's about who you know. And let me tell you, the community of collectors and enthusiasts out there is a veritable goldmine of knowledge, connections, and, most importantly, tip offs about the latest and greatest vintage finds.

Start by immersing yourself in the local retro tech scene – attend those quaint little electronics fairs, frequent the mom and-pop repair shops, and don't be afraid to strike up a conversation with the fellow geeks browsing the aisles. You never know who might let slip the location of a secret stash of vintage Walkmans or the name of that collector who's looking to offload their entire Commodore 64 collection.

And speaking of collectors, don't be shy about reaching out and connecting with them directly. Join the online forums, engage with the social media groups, and make yourself a known presence in the community. These folks are often more than willing to share their expertise, point you toward valuable resources, and even cut you in on the occasional exclusive deal. After all, what's the point of hoarding all that retro tech knowledge and insider information if you can't spread the wealth?

Remember, in the world of retro tech, it's not just about the hunt – it's about the camaraderie, the shared passion, and the thrill of discovering those hidden gems together. So get out there, network like a pro, and watch your retro tech riches start to pile up!

Storing and Preserving Your Finds

Proper Packaging and Transportation

Ah, the thrill of the hunt! You've scoured the thrift stores, flea markets, and garage sales, and now you've amassed a collection of vintage electronics that would make even the most seasoned collector drool. But before you start counting your profits, you need to ensure that your precious finds are properly stored and transported, lest they end up in a sorry state.

First and foremost, invest in quality packaging materials. Sturdy cardboard boxes, bubble wrap, and packing peanuts are your best friends. Treat each item with the care and attention it deserves, meticulously wrapping and cushioning it to prevent any damage during the journey from your thrifting adventures to your storage space. Trust me, you don't want to open a box only to find a once pristine vintage radio reduced to a pile of shattered parts.

When it comes to transportation, be mindful of the conditions. Avoid exposing your treasures to extreme temperatures, moisture, or direct sunlight. Pack them securely in your vehicle, and consider using climate controlled storage units or your own climate controlled space if you're transporting larger items. Remember, these vintage electronics are delicate and susceptible to the elements, so treat them with the utmost care.

As you navigate the winding roads of retro tech thrifting, think of your precious cargo as priceless antiques. With the right packaging and transportation techniques, you can ensure that your finds maintain their value and preserve their timeless allure for years to come.

Climate Controlled Storage Solutions

Once you've safely transported your vintage electronics, the next step is to provide them with a proper home. Enter the world of climate controlled storage solutions – your vintage tech's best friend.

Vintage electronics are notoriously sensitive to environmental factors, and that's where climate controlled storage shines. Invest in a dedicated space, whether it's a spare room in your home or a rental unit, that can maintain consistent temperature and humidity levels. This helps prevent the dreaded enemy of retro tech: corrosion, mold, and other environmental damages that can quickly turn your prized possessions into worthless relics.

When setting up your climate controlled storage, pay close attention to the temperature and humidity levels. Aim for a comfortable range, typically between 65 75°F (18 24°C) and 40 50% relative humidity. Fluctuations in these conditions can wreak havoc on delicate components and finishes, so strive for stability.

Don't forget to invest in proper shelving and storage systems, too. Sturdy, adjustable shelves allow you to organize your collection, while airtight containers or display cases can further protect your items from dust, pests, and the ravages of time. With a bit of planning and some climate control magic, your vintage electronics will be well on their way to a long and prosperous future.

Maintaining the Integrity of Your Collection

Congratulations, you've mastered the art of packaging and storage! But your job doesn't end there. Maintaining the integrity of your vintage electronics collection requires ongoing attention and care. After all, you're not just dealing with mere gadgets – these are living, breathing pieces of history that deserve your utmost respect.

Regularly inspect your collection for any signs of wear, tear, or degradation. Keep a watchful eye on those delicate capacitors, crumbling rubber seals, and tarnished metal surfaces. At the first sign of trouble, address it swiftly. Consult repair manuals, forums, or even local restoration experts to ensure you're taking the proper steps to preserve your treasures.

Gentle cleaning is also essential. Use soft, lint free cloths and approved cleaning solutions to gently wipe down surfaces and components. Avoid harsh chemicals or abrasives that could further damage the original finishes and materials. Embrace the patina – that's what gives these vintage gems their irresistible charm!

And don't forget the importance of documentation. Maintain detailed records of each item in your collection, including its history, condition, and any repairs or modifications you've made. This information will not only help you in your own research and selling efforts, but it also ensures that your precious cargo is well cared for, even in the event of an unforeseen transfer of ownership.

By following these guidelines, you'll be well on your way to becoming a trusted steward of vintage electronics, safeguarding these technological marvels for generations to come. So, dust off your gloves, roll up your sleeves, and get ready to begin on a journey of preservation and appreciation for the retro tech that captivates us all.

Researching and Pricing Your Inventory

Utilizing Online Resources and Price Guides

Welcome aboard, fellow retro tech enthusiasts! Now that you've amassed a goldmine of vintage electronics, it's time to dive deeper into the art of research and pricing. Believe me, this is where the real fun begins. No more scavenging thrift stores like a herd of hungry raccoons - now you get to channel your inner Sherlock Holmes and uncover the hidden gems in your collection.

First things first, let's talk about those trusty online resources and price guides. These are the digital breadcrumbs that will lead you straight to retro tech riches. Forget about the outdated tomes gathering dust on your shelves – the internet is where the real action is. Hop on those forums, scour the virtual flea markets, and immerse yourself in the vibrant online communities of fellow collectors and resellers.

Platforms like eBay, Craigslist, and Facebook Marketplace are goldmines of intel. Meticulously comb through past sold listings, not just the current asking prices. This will give you a deep understanding of the true market value of your vintage electronics. And don't forget about those specialized price guides – they're like the secret decoder rings of the retro tech world.

But here's the real kicker: don't just passively consume this information. Use it to your advantage! Become a master of cross referencing and pattern recognition. Spot the trends, the hidden gems, the outliers. This is where the magic happens, my friends. Embrace your inner data nerd and let those analytical juices flow.

Evaluating Rarity and Collectibility

Alright, now that you've armed yourself with a wealth of pricing data, it's time to put on your detective hat and really dive into the nitty gritty of your vintage electronics. Rarity and collectibility are the holy grail of the retro tech world, and trust me, these factors can make or break your bottom line.

Start by getting up close and personal with your finds. Examine those serial numbers, model designations, and any unique features that set them apart from the common crowd. Scour the internet for obscure product histories, limited production runs, and discontinued models. Become a walking encyclopedia of retro tech trivia – your knowledge could be the difference between a measly sale and a life changing payday.

And let's not forget about the condition and originality of your items. A pristine, untouched vintage speaker will always command a higher price than a well loved, modified one. But don't be too quick to dismiss those well loved beauties – sometimes, a little retro patina is exactly what collectors crave. The key is to highlight the unique story behind each piece, whether it's a mint condition marvel or a well traveled vintage wonder.

Ah, but the real secret sauce? Networking, my friends. Connecting with other enthusiasts, collectors, and industry experts can give you an indispensable edge. Tap into that hive mind, pick their brains, and uncover the hidden gems that the masses have yet to discover. Trust me, a little elbow grease and a whole lot of passion can take you further than any price guide ever will.

Determining the Right Selling Price

Alright, time to put all that research and evaluation to work – it's pricing time! But hold on to your vintage hats, because this isn't your typical "slap a price tag on it and call it a day" scenario. Nah, this is where the true art of the deal comes into play.

First and foremost, resist the urge to get greedy. Sure, you want to maximize your profits, but let's not lose sight of the bigger picture. Remember, you're not just selling a piece of hardware – you're selling a story, an experience, a connection to the past. Price it too high, and you might scare away your loyal fans. Price it too low, and you'll be kicking yourself all the way to the bank.

The key is to strike that delicate balance – one part cold, hard data, one part gut instinct. Scour those price guides, analyze the competition, and keep a close eye on the ebb and flow of the market. But don't forget to factor in the unique quirks and characteristics of your vintage treasures. That one of-a kind, custom modded Walkman? Yeah, that's not your average yard sale find, my friend.

And let's not forget about the power of perceived value.

Sometimes, the secret to commanding top dollar lies in the way you present your items. Craft those listings with a deft touch, highlighting the history, the rarity, the sheer awesomeness of your vintage electronics. Embrace your inner wordsmith and let your passion shine through. After all, you're not just selling a product – you're selling a piece of history.

Selling on Online Marketplaces

Setting Up Selling Accounts and Profiles

Alright, let's dive into the world of online marketplaces and get your retro tech selling game on the fast track. First things first, you'll need to set up your selling accounts and profiles. Now, I know what you're thinking - "But there are so many options, how do I choose?" Fear not, my friend, for I am about to bestow upon you the secrets of the digital selling elite.

eBay, Etsy, Facebook Marketplace - these are the holy trinity of online platforms for retro tech aficionados. Each one has its own unique quirks and specialties, so it's essential to pick the right one (or ones) that harmonize with your products and target audience. Are you dealing in rare and valuable vintage gadgets? eBay is your jam. Focused on the quirkier, artsy side of retro tech? Etsy is where you'll find your people. And if you're looking to tap into the local community, Facebook Marketplace is the way to go.

Don't be afraid to experiment and diversify your selling channels. After all, the more platforms you're on, the more opportunities you'll have to reach potential buyers. Just be prepared to become a master of juggling multiple accounts, listings, and customer inquiries. It's like being a circus performer, but with less sequins and more soldering irons.

Now, when it comes to your selling profiles, think of it as

your digital storefront. You want it to be eye catching, informative, and oozing with personality. Craft a killer bio that showcases your expertise in the retro tech world, sprinkle in some witty one liners, and don't forget to include high quality photos of your inventory. Remember, first impressions count, so make sure your profiles are as polished as the vintage electronics you're selling.

Crafting Effective Listings and Descriptions

Alright, now that your selling accounts are set up and ready to go, it's time to put on your marketing hat and start crafting those listings. Listen up, because this is where the real magic happens. Your listings are the digital storefront that will entice buyers to click, swoon, and ultimately, open their wallets.

Start with a captivating title that packs a punch. Think along the lines of "Rare 1980s Atari 2600 - Perfectly Preserved Gem" or "Vintage Sony Walkman - The Ultimate Retro Jukebox." Keep it concise, but make sure it grabs attention and clearly communicates the essence of your product.

Now, let's talk about the descriptions. This is where you really get to flex your creative muscles and let your inner wordsmith shine. Ditch the boring, cookie cutter approach and instead, weave a compelling narrative that transports your potential buyers back in time. Describe the history, the condition, and the sheer nostalgia factor of your retro tech finds. Sprinkle in a few quirky anecdotes or fun facts to make it truly memorable.

But don't forget the practical details, either. Meticulously list all the specifications, features, and any potential flaws or issues. Transparency is key when it comes to vintage electronics - after all, you want your buyers to be just as excited about their purchase as you are.

And, of course, don't forget to include high quality, well lit photos that showcase your items from every angle. These images will be the visual representation of your products, so make sure they're nothing short of stunning.

Managing Shipping and Customer Service

Alright, now that you've got your listings dialed in and your digital storefront is looking like a retro tech wonderland, it's time to tackle the next critical piece of the puzzle: shipping and customer service. This is where the rubber meets the road, my friend, so buckle up.

First, let's talk shipping. Investing in the right packaging and shipping materials is essential when it comes to safely transporting your vintage electronics. We're talking sturdy boxes, plenty of cushioning, and a healthy dose of bubble wrap (or better yet, those cool air filled pockets that are almost as satisfying to pop as bubble wrap). Trust me, you don't want your prized 1970s Walkman to arrive at its new home looking like it went through a blender.

And speaking of that new home, your shipping process needs to be lightning fast and efficient. Nobody wants to wait weeks for their retro tech treasure to arrive. Offer a range of shipping options, from lightning fast express delivery to good old fashioned snail mail for the more budget conscious buyers. Just make sure to communicate those options clearly in your listings and be upfront about any potential delays or shipping challenges.

Now, let's talk about customer service. In the world of online selling, your buyers are the lifeblood of your business, so you'd better treat them like royalty. Be prompt, friendly, and above all, solution oriented. If a customer has a question, a concern, or (heaven forbid) a return, approach it with a positive attitude and a willingness to go the extra mile.

Respond to inquiries quickly, be transparent about your policies, and do everything in your power to ensure a fluid and satisfying buying experience. After all, a happy customer is not only more likely to leave glowing reviews, but they're also more likely to come back and become a loyal member of your retro tech selling empire.

Selling at Retro Tech Fairs and Conventions

Navigating Vendor Applications and Fees

When it comes to hawking your vintage tech treasures, there's no better place to be than the hallowed halls of a retro tech fair or convention. But before you can start raking in the big bucks, you've got to navigate the often byzantine world of vendor applications and fees. It's enough to make your inner tech geek short circuit, but fear not, my fellow hustlers – we've got your back.

First things first, do your homework. Scour the event websites, dig through social media, and network with seasoned vendors to uncover the nitty gritty details. Some events have strict criteria for who can sell, while others are more of a free for-all. Make sure your vintage wares fit the bill, and be prepared to jump through the necessary hoops – trust me, it's worth it to avoid any last minute headaches.

Now, let's talk fees. These can range from a couple of bucks for a table at a small community swap meet to hundreds, even thousands, for a prime spot at a major convention. Don't let the sticker shock scare you off, though. Think of it as an investment in your retro tech empire – the potential payoff is well worth the cost of admission.

One insider tip? Negotiate, negotiate, negotiate. Many event organizers are willing to cut deals, especially for first timers or those with a killer vintage collection. Offer to volunteer or help with setup, or see if they'll throw in some extra perks like access to exclusive pre sale hours. The more you can sweeten the pot, the better your chances of scoring a sweet deal.

Presenting and Displaying Your Items

Alright, you've conquered the vendor application process and secured your spot at the big show. Now comes the fun part: showtime! But before you start piling your vintage wares on the table, take a step back and consider your display strategy. After all, you're not just selling products – you're selling an experience, a piece of nostalgia that's going to captivate your customers and have them reaching for their wallets faster than you can say "Betamax."

First things first, invest in some quality display fixtures. Forget the rickety card tables and flimsy shelves – you want to create a sense of elegance and sophistication. Think sleek, modern stands that showcase your items in the best possible light. And don't be afraid to get a little creative – maybe a vintage inspired light box or a retro themed backdrop to really set the mood.

Next, arrange your items with the care and precision of a museum curator. Group similar items together, create eye catching vignettes, and make sure every piece is visible and accessible. And don't forget the power of storytelling – add little placards or labels that share the history and significance of your vintage treasures. Trust me, your customers will eat it up.

Finally, keep your display dynamic and engaging. Rotate

your inventory, change up the layouts, and don't be afraid to get a little theatrical. Maybe you'll have a working vintage TV playing classic commercials, or a retro inspired photo booth where customers can capture their own slice of tech nostalgia. The more you can immerse your buyers in the experience, the more likely they are to walk away with a piece of your vintage tech magic.

Engaging with Buyers and Collectors

Now that you've got your vendor booth looking like a million bucks, it's time to put on your salesman hat and start charming the socks off your potential customers. But this isn't your average hard sell – no, this is all about building authentic connections and nurturing a loyal following of retro tech enthusiasts.

First and foremost, be approachable and engaged. Don't hide behind your display – get out there, shake some hands, and strike up conversations. Ask about your buyers' interests, their collections, and what they're hoping to find. The more you can learn about them, the better you'll be able to match them with the perfect vintage treasure.

And speaking of treasure, be a font of knowledge. Share the backstories and quirky details about your items – the more you can get your customers excited about the history and significance, the more they'll be willing to part with their hard earned cash. Just make sure you strike the right balance between informative and entertaining – you want to captivate, not overwhelm.

Of course, the real magic happens when you can tap into

that shared passion for all things retro tech. Perhaps you'll bond over a mutual love of vintage oscilloscopes, or swap stories about the first time you booted up an old school gaming console. These connections are pure gold, not just for making a sale, but for building long term relationships with your most dedicated collectors.

So don't be afraid to get a little weird and wacky – after all, that's what the retro tech scene is all about. Embrace your inner tech nerd, let your enthusiasm shine, and watch as your customers become lifelong fans. Who knows, you might even make a few friends along the way. Now go forth, my fellow hustlers, and let the retro tech selling commence!

Building Your Retro Tech Brand

Developing a Unique Selling Proposition

In the vast and ever evolving world of retro tech, standing out from the crowd is vital. Your vintage electronics business needs to offer something truly unique to capture the hearts and wallets of detecting collectors and enthusiasts. Forget about trying to be the "jack of all trades" - instead, focus on becoming the master of a niche. Whether it's specializing in rare gaming consoles, curating a collection of iconic audio equipment, or offering top notch restoration services, carving out your own specialized territory will be the key to building a loyal customer base.

Start by examining your passions and expertise within the retro tech realm. What era or brand excites you the most? What unique skills or knowledge do you possess that others may lack? Embrace your inner geek and let that passion shine through in everything you do. Develop a clear and compelling brand identity that reflects your distinctive personality and expertise. Craft a catchy tagline, design a visually striking logo, and infuse your marketing materials with a touch of retro flair.

But don't stop there. Go beyond the surface level branding and truly immerse yourself in the retro tech community. Attend local meetups, join online forums, and connect with other collectors and enthusiasts. Become a trusted source of knowledge, offering valuable realizations, restoration tips, and collector focused content. Position yourself as an authority in your niche, and your customers will flock to you as the go to expert in the field.

Leveraging Social Media and Online Presence

In the digital age, your online presence is the gateway to reaching and engaging your target audience. Social media platforms have become the ultimate battleground for retro tech enthusiasts, and mastering this arena can be a game changer for your business.

Start by carefully selecting the social channels that match best with your brand and target market. Instagram and YouTube may be ideal for showcasing your beautifully curated vintage electronics, while Facebook and Reddit communities can provide valuable networking opportunities and customer perceptions. Consistently post high quality, visually striking content that captures the essence of your brand and connects with your followers.

But don't just post and pray. Engage with your audience, respond to comments, and encourage a sense of community around your brand. Share behind the-scenes glimpses of your thrifting adventures, offer restoration tutorials, and invite your followers to share their own retro tech stories. The more you can humanize your brand and connect with your customers on a personal level, the more loyal and devoted they will become.

Complement your social media efforts with a polished, user friendly website that showcases your inventory, highlights your unique selling proposition, and provides a continuous shopping experience. Employ search engine optimization (SEO) tactics to ensure your online presence is easily discoverable by potential customers searching for vintage electronics. Invest in professional product photography, create engaging content, and make it easy for collectors to find and purchase the rare gems they covet.

Promoting a Loyal Customer Base

In the dynamic world of retro tech, building a loyal customer base is the key to sustainable success. These devoted collectors and enthusiasts are the backbone of your business, and nurturing their loyalty can uncover a world of opportunities.

Start by providing an exceptional customer experience from the very first interaction. Respond to inquiries promptly, offer personalized recommendations, and go above and beyond to ensure your customers feel valued and appreciated. Develop a VIP program that rewards your most dedicated patrons with exclusive access to rare finds, early access to new inventory, or special discounts.

Employ the power of community building to encourage a sense of belonging among your customer base. Organize meetups, workshops, or virtual events where your customers can connect, share stories, and even participate in friendly trading or restoration sessions. Encourage user generated content, such as customer showcase posts or restoration project updates, to build a sense of shared passion and camaraderie.

Keep your finger on the pulse of the retro tech market by constantly engaging with your customers. Solicit feedback, ask for suggestions, and involve them in the decision making process. This not only demonstrates your commitment to their needs but also helps you stay ahead of the curve and anticipate the next big trends in the industry.

Remember, in the world of retro tech, your customers aren't just buyers – they're true enthusiasts who share your love for these vintage gems. By nurturing that connection and making them feel like an vital part of your brand, you'll grow a loyal following that will propel your business to new heights.

Scaling Your Retro Tech Business

Expanding Your Inventory and Sourcing

Congratulations, your retro tech business is starting to gain some serious momentum! But don't get too comfortable just yet - it's time to kick things into high gear and really start scaling those operations. The first step? Expanding your inventory and sourcing game. Gone are the days of haphazardly scavenging thrift stores and begging your great aunt for her old Betamax collection. No, my friend, it's time to get strategic.

Start by diversifying your sourcing channels. Sure, the thrill of the hunt at garage sales and flea markets is unparalleled, but you need to broaden your horizons. Start networking with other collectors, join online forums, and even consider reaching out to estate sale companies. Those old timers have a knack for unearthing hidden gems that would make your vintage calculator collection blush.

And speaking of collectors, don't be afraid to get a little...creative with your acquisition methods. Maybe offer to trade that mint condition Walkman you scored for a rare laserdisc player. Or, heck, why not try your hand at bartering? I once traded a box of vintage Atari cartridges for a classic Polaroid camera and a slightly used fondue set. Don't knock it till you try it, am I right?

But let's not forget the digital realm, either. Scour online marketplaces, auction sites, and even manufacturer liquidations for those hidden gems. Just make sure you've done your homework - research prices, condition, and rarity before pulling the trigger. Nothing stings quite like realizing you overpaid for a "rare" 8 track player that's actually a dime a dozen.

Automating and Streamlining Processes

As your retro tech empire grows, so too will the mountain of tasks on your to do list. Cleaning, testing, pricing, listing, shipping - it can all add up in a hurry. That's why it's time to start automating and streamlining your processes. Trust me, your future self will thank you.

First, take a hard look at your inventory management system. Is it still a disorganized jumble of spreadsheets and sticky notes? Time for an upgrade, my friend. Invest in a dedicated inventory management software that can track your stock, generate reports, and even help you forecast demand. Bonus points if it integrates with your online selling platforms.

Speaking of online selling, make sure you've optimized your listings to the nines. Crafting engaging product descriptions and eye catching photos is one thing, but have you tapped into the power of automation? Look into tools that can automatically relist items, adjust prices based on market trends, and even handle customer inquiries and order fulfillment.

And let's not forget about the nuts and bolts of your business - things like bookkeeping, tax prep, and shipping logistics.

Sure, you could spend hours hunched over a calculator and piles of receipts, but why not outsource those tasks to the experts? Hire an accountant, apply a fulfillment service, and let the professionals handle the nitty gritty so you can focus on the fun stuff.

Diversifying Your Product Selections

Alright, you've got your inventory dialed in and your processes streamlined to the max. Now it's time to really take your retro tech business to the next level: diversification. Remember, variety is the spice of life, and the same goes for building a thriving entrepreneurial enterprise.

Sure, vintage electronics will always be your bread and butter, but why not explore adjacent product categories that can complement your core products? Start thinking outside the box - how about vintage audio equipment, classic video games, or even retro inspired home decor? The possibilities are endless, and the key is to stay flexible and adaptable.

But diversification doesn't just mean expanding your product line. It can also mean tapping into new sales channels and distribution networks. Maybe it's time to dip your toes into the world of brick and-mortar retail by renting a booth at a local flea market or antique mall. Or perhaps you could explore wholesale opportunities, selling your curated vintage wares to other resellers and collectors.

The bottom line is this: don't let your retro tech business become a one trick pony. Constantly explore new avenues for growth, and be willing to take calculated risks. Who knows, that random impulse purchase of a truckload of vintage RadioShack accessories might just end up being your next big moneymaker. The only way to find out is to keep that entrepreneurial spirit alive and kicking.

Navigating Legal and Tax Considerations

Understanding Seller Regulations and Licenses

Ah, the joys of navigating the legal terrain as a retro tech thrifter and reseller. Just when you thought you'd mastered the art of finding rare gems and restoring them to their former glory, you realize there's a whole other world of red tape and bureaucracy waiting to trip you up. But fear not, my fellow vintage electronic enthusiasts, for we shall conquer this obstacle course with the grace and finesse of a Commodore 64 speedrunner.

First and foremost, let's address the elephant in the room – licenses. Depending on your location and the scope of your retro tech business, you may need to obtain various permits and licenses to operate legally. Research the requirements in your area, and be prepared to don your best "I'm totally-not a-secret agent" disguise as you navigate the bureaucratic maze. Remember, the more forms you can fill out in invisible ink, the better.

Now, let's talk about sales tax. This is the bane of every thrifter's existence, but fear not, for the power of spreadsheets and calculator apps shall be your allies. Keep meticulous records of your transactions, and be prepared to collect and remit sales tax to the appropriate authorities. Imagine the thrill of watching your accounting spreadsheet transform into a work of art, with columns and rows that could make an accountant weep with joy.

And let's not forget about the ever elusive customs and import regulations. If you're sourcing your vintage electronics from overseas, be prepared to navigate a minefield of paperwork and arcane rules. Just picture yourself as a cyber punk hacker, breaching the firewalls of international bureaucracy to secure your precious haul of retro tech treasures.

Properly Reporting Income and Expenses

As a savvy retro tech entrepreneur, you've probably already mastered the art of creative accounting. But let's take it to the next level, shall we? When it comes to reporting your income and expenses, think of yourself as a modern day alchemist, transforming the mundane into the extraordinary.

Start by keeping meticulous records of your every transaction, from the pennies you shelled out for that hidden gem at the local thrift store to the princely sums you raked in from your online marketplace sales. Embrace the power of spreadsheets and accounting software, but don't be afraid to add a little personal touch – perhaps a few doodles of your favorite vintage consoles in the margins, just to keep things interesting.

When it comes time to file your taxes, channel your inner Sherlock Holmes and scour every nook and cranny for potential deductions. Did you spend hours restoring that rare Atari console? Write it off as a business expense. Need to purchase a climate controlled storage unit to house your growing collection? Cha ching, another deduction. Just remember to keep your receipts in order, lest you find yourself in the crosshairs of the dreaded tax authorities.

And if all else fails, remember the immortal words of that legendary tech innovator, Al Capone: "The trick is not to get caught." Okay, maybe not those exact words, but you get the idea. Approach your financial reporting with the same cunning and resourcefulness that you apply to your retro tech sourcing and sales.

Protecting Yourself from Liability

Now, let's talk about the unthinkable – liability. As a retro tech entrepreneur, the last thing you want is to find yourself in a tangled web of legal troubles, all because of a malfunctioning vintage radio that someone claims gave them a nasty shock (or, heaven forbid, a case of the giggles).

First and foremost, ensure that you've got the proper insurance coverage in place. We're talking comprehensive liability insurance, product liability insurance, and maybe even a little something called "Oops, I accidentally let loose a swarm of mutant cassette tapes" coverage (okay, maybe not that last one, but you get the idea).

But insurance alone won't save you – you've got to be proactive in your approach to liability. Implement rigorous testing and quality control measures for every vintage electronic you sell. Carefully document every step of your restoration and repair process, and be prepared to provide detailed records to any potential litigants. It's like building a digital fortress around your business, complete with laser guided security cameras and a squad of robotic guards (or, you know, just a well organized filing system).

And don't forget about the power of the legal disclaimer. Craft your sales listings and contracts with the precision of a master swordsmith, using words that could make even the most litigious customer think twice before trying to sue you. Imagine your listings as a labyrinth of legalese, with each clause a trap that would leave even the most determined lawyer scratching their head in bewilderment.

Remember, the world of retro tech may be your playground, but it's also a minefield of potential legal landmines. Arm yourself with knowledge, vigilance, and a healthy dose of mischievous charm, and you'll be well on your way to navigating the treacherous waters of liability with the grace and agility of a vintage Atari Pong back.

Outsourcing and Partnerships

Leveraging Dropshipping and Fulfillment Services

In the high octane world of retro tech trading, you've gotta be nimble, my friend. That's where the magic of dropshipping and fulfillment services comes into play. Imagine this: you list a vintage Atari 2600 on your online store, and the next thing you know, BING, it's sold! But instead of scrambling to pack that baby up and ship it off, you simply let your trusted fulfillment partner handle the whole shebang. They'll take care of the pick, pack, and ship, freeing you up to focus on the real money making stuff - like scouring thrift stores for your next rare gem.

Now, I know what you're thinking - "But Vinny, won't that cut into my profits?" Au contraire, my friend. By outsourcing the logistics, you can keep your overhead low and your margins high. Plus, these fulfillment wizards have the connections and infrastructure to get your items to their new owners faster and more efficiently than you could ever manage solo. It's a win win, I tell ya.

And let's not forget about the dropshipping angle. Instead of stockpiling your inventory in a basement that's slowly turning into a retro tech version of the Collyer brothers' place, you can partner with suppliers who'll handle the storage and shipping for you. All you gotta do is list the items, and when they sell, the supplier takes care of the rest.

Boom, just like that, you're a lean, mean, vintage electronics slingin' machine.

Of course, you've gotta vet these partners carefully. Make sure they've got a solid track record, lightning fast turnaround times, and a commitment to preserving the integrity of your vintage goods. And don't be afraid to negotiate – these folks are in the business of making money, just like you, so use that to your advantage.

Collaborating with Repair Specialists

Now, let's talk about another key partnership in the retro tech game: the repair specialists. These are the unsung heroes who can take a busted up, forgotten about piece of vintage tech and bring it back to life like some kind of electronic Frankenstein. And trust me, you want these folks in your corner.

When you stumble upon a rare find at a thrift store or garage sale, it might be tempting to slap a "as is" label on it and hope for the best. But that's a risky move, my friends. One wrong turn of a knob or a faulty capacitor, and your potential goldmine could turn into a lead lined paperweight. That's where your repair specialist comes in.

Build relationships with the local tinkerers, the electronics whizzes, the guys (and gals) who can diagnose and fix anything from a 1970s stereo receiver to a 1980s computer. These folks are worth their weight in vintage transistors, let me tell you. Not only can they revive your treasures, but they can also help you assess the condition and value of your finds, ensuring you don't overpay or underestimate the true worth of your inventory.

Plus, by partnering with repair specialists, you can offer a more comprehensive service to your customers. Imagine being able to sell a fully restored and tested vintage console, complete with a warranty and the peace of mind that comes with knowing it's in tip top shape. That's the kind of value that'll have your buyers lining up like it's Black Friday at the Sharper Image.

Just be sure to vet these specialists as thoroughly as your fulfillment partners. Look for folks with a proven track record, a passion for vintage tech, and the patience of a saint. After all, you're trusting them with your most prized possessions – you want to make sure they'll treat them with the care and respect they deserve.

Forging Mutually Beneficial Relationships

In the world of retro tech, the real power lies in the connections you make. It's not just about who you know, but how you make use of those relationships to create a thriving, sustainable business. And when it comes to partnerships, the key is to approach them with a win win mentality.

Think about it – you've got your fulfillment wizards, your repair specialists, and a whole host of other potential collaborators out there. Instead of viewing them as competitors or simply as service providers, see them as allies in your quest for retro tech riches. After all, you're all in this game for the same reason: a deep, abiding love for the vintage electronics of yesteryear.

So, how do you build these mutually beneficial relationships? Start by being the kind of partner you'd want to work with yourself. Show up with a genuine interest in their business, their expertise, and their passions. Share knowledge, swap war stories, and find ways to help them grow just as much as you're helping yourself.

Maybe you can introduce your repair specialist to a new supplier of hard to-find vintage components. Or perhaps you can hook up your fulfillment partner with a client who's looking to scale their retro tech e commerce operation. The key is to think creatively, to always be on the lookout for opportunities to add value, and to remember that a rising tide lifts all boats.

And don't forget the power of reciprocity. When your partners succeed, find ways to celebrate and support them. Refer new clients their way, shout them out on your social channels, or even collaborate on a joint venture. The more you can make them feel like they're an vital part of your business network, the more they'll be invested in your success – and the more you'll all thrive in the ever changing world of retro tech.

Maintaining a Sustainable Retro Tech Business

Adapting to Market Trends and Changes

In the ever evolving world of retro tech, the ability to adapt and stay ahead of the curve is very important. Gone are the days when you could simply hoard your vintage finds and expect them to appreciate in value indefinitely. Nope, this ain't your grandpa's flea market empire – this is the wild, unpredictable realm of tech nostalgia, where trends can shift faster than a malfunctioning Commodore 64 on a bad day.

So, how do you keep your retro tech business thriving in the face of such uncertainty? First and foremost, you need to become a borderline obsessive market researcher. Scour forums, trawl social media, and befriend every retro tech enthusiast with a pulse. Trust me, those guys know more about the latest collectible Walkman models than the engineers who made them.

But don't just sit back and wait for the trends to hit you in the face – be proactive, my friend. Experiment with new product categories, test the waters with different marketing tactics, and always, *always* be on the lookout for the next big thing. Who knows, maybe that dusty old Atari 2600 you scored at a garage sale will be the hottest item on the block next year.

And let's not forget about the ever evolving world of technology itself. Keep a close eye on the latest advancements in retro gaming emulators, restoration techniques, and even 3D printing. Embrace these innovations, incorporate them into your business model, and watch as your customers flock to you like moths to a neon lit Pac Man cabinet.

Preventing Burnout and Stress Management

Ah, the double edged sword of the retro tech entrepreneur – the thrill of the hunt, the rush of a successful sale, the satisfaction of seeing your collection grow. But with great vintage finds come great responsibility, and if you're not careful, that passion can quickly turn into a never ending grind that leaves you burned out and in desperate need of a digital detox.

The key to avoiding this pitfall? Learn to strike a balance, my friend. Sure, it's tempting to spend every waking hour scouring thrift stores and scouring online marketplaces for the next rare gem, but trust me, your mental health (and your social life) will thank you for taking a step back.

Implement strict work life boundaries, and don't be afraid to delegate tasks or outsource when the workload becomes overwhelming. Carve out time for yourself, whether it's a weekend getaway to a retro tech convention or simply an evening spent tinkering with your favorite vintage console. And don't forget the importance of self care – exercise, healthy eating, and good old fashioned rest and relaxation can do wonders for your productivity and overall well being.

Remember, burnout is the enemy of sustained success. By taking a proactive approach to stress management, you'll be able to maintain the energy and enthusiasm that made you fall in love with the retro tech hustle in the first place.

Reinvesting and Diversifying Your Income Streams

Alright, let's talk money, honey. Because let's face it, as much as we love the thrill of the hunt and the joy of preserving vintage tech, at the end of the day, this is a business – and a profitable one, if you play your cards right.

The key to long term sustainability? Reinvesting your hard earned profits back into your operation. I'm talking about upgrading your storage solutions, investing in high quality photography equipment, and perhaps even expanding into new product categories or services.

But don't just stop at reinvestment – it's time to get that diversification game on lock. After all, who knows when the next big retro tech trend will come and go? Spread your wings, my friend, and explore other revenue streams that complement your core business.

Maybe you could offer restoration services, teaching workshops on vintage electronics repair, or even dabble in the world of retro tech consulting. Heck, you could even start your own line of custom designed retro inspired accessories – the possibilities are endless!

And let's not forget about the ever evolving world of online marketplaces and selling platforms. Stay on top of the latest trends, experiment with different approaches, and be willing to adapt your strategy as the terrain changes. After all, the key to a thriving retro tech business is the ability to think outside the (CRT) box.

Giving Back to the Retro Tech Community

Sharing Knowledge and Expertise

As you've delved into the captivating world of vintage electronics, you've undoubtedly amassed a wealth of knowledge and expertise. It would be a shame to hoard all that juicy information for yourself, wouldn't it? After all, the true reward of this journey isn't just the thrill of the hunt or the satisfaction of a lucrative sale - it's the camaraderie and shared passion that comes with being part of the retro tech community.

So, why not put on your teacher's hat and start sharing your hard earned wisdom with others? Whether it's through engaging blog posts, informative YouTube tutorials, or interactive workshops, your unique perspective and observations could be priceless to aspiring retro tech enthusiasts and budding entrepreneurs. Imagine the look on someone's face when you reveal the secret to spotting a rare Commodore 64 amidst a sea of thrift store clutter. Priceless!

Don't be afraid to get creative with your knowledge sharing endeavors. Maybe you could start a podcast where you interview veteran collectors and share their stories. Or perhaps you could host a live Q&A session on a popular online forum, fielding questions from newbies and seasoned pros alike. The possibilities are endless, and the payoff is twofold: not only will you be helping to nurture the next generation of retro tech aficionados, but you'll also be cementing your status as a trusted authority in the community.

Organizing Workshops and Meetups

Imagine a world where like minded individuals can gather to geek out over vintage electronics, swap war stories, and trade prized possessions. Well, my friend, that world is yours to create. By organizing workshops and meetups, you have the power to grow a thriving community of retro tech enthusiasts, bringing together collectors, restoration experts, and aspiring entrepreneurs under one roof.

Start by tapping into your local network – reach out to fellow thrifters, flea market regulars, and even the owners of vintage electronics shops. See if they'd be interested in collaborating on a hands on workshop where participants can learn the art of restoring a classic Atari console or the proper techniques for cleaning and preserving a vintage Walkman. Offering these kinds of interactive experiences not only nurtures a sense of camaraderie but also helps to educate and inspire the next generation of retro tech enthusiasts.

But don't stop there! Take your community building efforts to the digital realm by organizing virtual meetups and online forums. These platforms allow you to connect with collectors and hobbyists from all over the world, sharing tips, trading stories, and even hosting virtual show and-tell sessions. Who knows – you might even spark a lively debate over the merits of the Sega Genesis versus the Super Nintendo. Just make sure to have the popcorn ready!

Supporting Preservation and Restoration Efforts

In the ever evolving terrain of technology, it's easy to forget the importance of preserving our retro tech heritage. But as a savvy thrifter and seller of vintage electronics, you understand the true value of these cultural artifacts. They're not just relics of a bygone era; they're windows into the past, reminders of the ingenuity and creativity that paved the way for the digital marvels we enjoy today.

That's why it's critical to lend your support to organizations and initiatives dedicated to the preservation and restoration of vintage electronics. Whether it's donating rare or hard to-find parts to a local repair workshop or volunteering your time and expertise to help revive a vintage computer, every little bit helps to ensure that these technological treasures continue to captivate and inspire future generations.

Perhaps you could even spearhead your own preservation project, such as establishing a community driven retro tech museum or creating an online database to catalog and document the unique stories behind these vintage machines. Imagine the joy on the face of a young visitor as they discover the magic of a Commodore 64 or the awe inspiring complication of a vintage oscilloscope. By sharing these experiences, you're not just preserving history - you're igniting a spark of wonder that could inspire the next generation of tech innovators.

Conclusion and Future Outlook

Embracing the Passion for Retro Tech

As we reach the end of our journey through the world of retro tech thrifting and selling, it's important to reflect on the passion that has driven us thus far. This pursuit is not merely about the numbers on a spreadsheet or the buzz of a new sale – it's about a deep rooted love for the artifacts of a bygone era. These vintage electronics, with their quirky designs and nostalgic charm, have the power to transport us back in time, to a simpler age where technology was not just a tool, but a captivating work of art.

Throughout this book, we've explored the thrill of the hunt, the satisfaction of restoring a forgotten treasure, and the joy of sharing these marvels with fellow enthusiasts. This passion is what sets us apart from mere opportunists – it's the driving force that keeps us scouring thrift stores, poring over price guides, and meticulously preserving our finds. As you continue on your retro tech journey, never lose sight of that spark, that innate curiosity that drew you to this field in the first place.

Embrace the passion, for it is the very lifeblood of your business. Allow it to guide your decisions, inspire your creativity, and fuel your determination. Let it be the North Star that illuminates the path ahead, even when the road grows long and the obstacles seem daunting. For in the end, it is this love for the past that will ensure the future of the retro tech industry.

Exploring Emerging Opportunities

The retro tech setting is ever evolving, and with it, new and exciting opportunities are constantly emerging. As the world becomes increasingly enamored with the charm and nostalgia of vintage electronics, the demand for these coveted items continues to soar. But the opportunities extend far beyond the simple act of buying and selling.

Consider the growing interest in restoration and preservation. More and more collectors and enthusiasts are seeking out skilled technicians and artisans who can breathe new life into these technological relics. By honing your expertise in vintage electronics repair and refurbishment, you can position yourself as a essential resource in this burgeoning market.

Another promising avenue is the integration of retro tech into modern design and decor. As the lines between the past and present become increasingly blurred, savvy entrepreneurs are finding creative ways to incorporate vintage electronics into contemporary spaces. From repurposed speakers to reimagined retro inspired tech accessories, the possibilities are truly endless.

Diversifying your selections by branching out into complementary product lines, such as retro inspired apparel, collectibles, or even educational workshops, can also open up new revenue streams and solidify your place within the retro tech community. The key is to keep a keen eye on emerging trends, stay nimble in your approach, and be willing to embrace the ever evolving nature of this dynamic industry.

Continuing Your Entrepreneurial Journey

As you reach the conclusion of this book, it's important to remember that your retro tech journey is far from over. In fact, this is just the beginning of an exhilarating entrepreneurial adventure, filled with endless possibilities and opportunities for growth.

The road ahead may not be smooth – there will be challenges to overcome, setbacks to navigate, and shifts to make. But it is these very obstacles that will test your resilience, sharpen your business acumen, and propel you towards even greater success. Embrace the uncertainty, for it is in the face of adversity that true innovation and creativity often thrive.

Remember, the retro tech community is not just a market – it's a vibrant system of passionate collectors, tinkerers, and aficionados. Immerse yourself in this world, build genuine connections, and use the collective knowledge and experience of your peers. Attend industry events, join online forums, and become an active participant in shaping the future of this captivating niche.

As you continue to expand your retro tech business, always strive to stay true to your vision and values. Let your passion for these vintage marvels guide your decision making, and never lose sight of the joy and satisfaction that this pursuit brings. By embracing the challenges, seizing the opportunities, and remaining steadfast in your commitment,

you can create a thriving, sustainable retro tech empire –
one that celebrates the enduring allure of the past while
paving the way for an exciting future.

Silas Meadowlark

www.ingramcontent.com/pod-product-compliance
Lightning Source LLC
Chambersburg PA
CBHW030048230526
45471CB00003B/998